Why Me?

My Fight for Life...

David M. Armstrong

Absolute Author
Publishing House

Why Me? My Fight for Life
Copyright © 2020 by David M. Armstrong
All Rights Reserved

Editor: Dr. Melissa Caudle
Junior Editor: Paul S. Dupre

Library of Congress Catalogue In-Publication-Data

Paperback ISBN: 978-1-64953-136-0

1. Self-help 2. Motivational 3. Men's Literature

DEDICATION

I dedicate this book to the millions of young men and women that need a reason to overcome the destiny that they've been thrown into as well as the mentors that find it in their kind hearts to dedicate time, energy and love to those that need it the most.

TABLE OF CONTENTS

Introduction

Imagine going through life absolutely and totally alone!

Take a moment to picture this emptiness; this isolation, this fear. "Life" is already full of challenges. That's why it's called "life," however, no one should face life completely alone, especially as a child. It makes you question, "**WHY**? Why me, what did I do, why my mom, my dad, my family?" Ultimately, you question, "Why do I even have to live?" It's an unfortunate reality that many youths in our world today have had to face, and that includes me as a young boy. What sets me apart from the unfortunate majority is that I'm here writing this book, an autobiography to help and inspire our youth who may be going through some of the situations that I would have had to encounter.

This book is intended to help and motivate individuals working with our youth as foster parents, teachers, ministers, youth correctional officers, judges, attorneys, social workers, and the youth with whom they are working. I hope my story helps you see that despite some of the situations "life" may throw at us...there is always a way.

David M. Armstrong

The Beginning

Some of us have very early childhood memories, and well, some of us have mentally blocked out a lot of our childhood experiences for various reasons. Maybe as a defense mechanism, an automatic, even programmed response by our body and brain. Sometimes we forget those bad memories that well; we just can't stand to keep replaying inside of our minds. I can't remember much before my father left the house when I was about seven years old, no matter how hard I try. I have a faint memory of him coming to the house... I yelled out, "Mom, Dad's here!" My mother responded, "Come here, don't open the door; he's not staying." My father came to the door where my mom had placed two packed suitcases, sitting outside on the porch. He grabbed the bags, and that was it. That was the last time I laid eyes on my father, and what a sad, unforgettable memory! I have no idea why he left and why he never came back into my life, but the feeling of abandonment had just started for young David and would get much worse. So, at that moment, he walked away from me for the last time. He got into his car and drove away.

There was a young woman in the passenger seat, and to this day, I have no clue who that girl was and why my mother wouldn't let me talk to him. I can only assume he was in some relationship with the girl, and both my mother and father had decided they needed to split up. But that's only my assumption. That scenario has been playing out, over and over, in my mind, for over twenty-five years. What am I missing - the why, the how, the what-ifs? Did I not deserve to have a father in my life to stick around to raise his son? Someone to teach me how to throw a football, a father to teach me about dating, a man to show me how to become a man? Did I not deserve this, or was it just my **destiny**? Abandonment is a horrible feeling! The truth is that most of us, luckily, have never honestly had this feeling. It's different from when a girlfriend and boyfriend break up suddenly. "Jack, this relationship isn't working out for me," says Jill, "it's not you; it's me." Yes, it hurts and can affect us in the short term and sometimes for a very long time. But, when it's a mother or father, the feeling lingers forever, no matter how much we try to block it from our mind or our life. It amplifies this feeling when we don't actually understand or know the circumstances of "Why?"

To those of us working with children, please understand that you most likely can never empathize with the children that have experienced this type of abandonment unless you have experienced it yourself. So, do yourself and everyone else a favor and do not compare it to something you've experienced, for example, a break-up or siblings who are not talking to each other for a long time. It's not the same, not even close! So, sympathize with these young men and women, and help them validate the feelings they might be experiencing and help them acknowledge that the situation had nothing to do with them, individually, and that, above all, acceptance is the best medicine.

Although I have a few good childhood memories of my mother and me, there aren't very many after my father left. My mom and I were very close, and I remember us playing around. We would wrestle, and she would joke with me all the time. I remember performing and dancing for my mother and her friends. I guess I liked to dance as a kid, well, even as an adult too, haha. I have wonderful memories of us going to the Rose Bowl Parade for Thanksgiving. It seemed like it was every year, for we would always camp outside the night before to get a "good spot" to watch the parade in the morning.

Thinking back now, I guess, for a while, we had a "normal" relationship for a young boy and his mother, as it was just she and I, the two of us, doing everything together. I'm not sure if we were rich, poor, or middle class. As far as income goes, I don't remember her going to work or being at daycare or anything like that. I do remember, though, some stories my mother would tell me about her childhood, her struggles to grow, and about her family. I also remember my sister being around occasionally. I know now that she's much older than I am, around eighteen years older or so. By the time I was of an age that I could remember things, she was out of the house, but I have no earthly clue "out" where. I've tried to find her several times, but with no luck. I think I found a daughter of hers a couple of years ago, but she said she doesn't speak with her mother - the woman that could be my sister - and she wouldn't do so even for me (update on my sister later). Even though I explained that her mother was most likely my long-lost sister, she didn't give a shit at all. Sad, how people can be, at times!!!

So, back to my mother. My mom had an unfortunate accident when she was a child. She fell down an elevator shaft. You know, the olden ones with the gate that had to be closed manually. Well, she fell down a few floors, blowing out both of her eardrums and subsequently losing her hearing in both ears. So, oddly enough, my first language was American sign language. It was the first "language" that I knew. Of course, I could speak, but I learned how to sign at the same time that I was learning how to speak, or so my mother told me. I remember needing to interpret for my mother all the time, but it wasn't such a bad thing. It was just everyday life for me to do so. I remember needing to communicate with "the hearing" for my mother outside of the house - at the grocery store, to buy medication, or to try to talk to just about any and everyone. It was extremely challenging to talk with individuals for my mother, on every given occasion, at such a young age. As I think about it now, it's a lot for a child, not even ten years old, to do. But I think that "responsibility" was preparing me for more life-impacting burdens that were waiting ahead for me to endure. It was slightly difficult for me to manage my mom being deaf.

As I grew older, kids would laugh and make fun of her, mumbling or imitating her speech. I even remember adults saying, "Oh, your mother is deaf and dumb," wow, dumb, why would she need to be dumb just because she can't hear? Her "deafness" started to become slightly embarrassing to me, but she was my mom, so, deep down inside, I didn't care what people would say. I remember being in school and kids teasing and making fun of my mother and how she spoke and taunted and said she was "deaf and dumb." Jesus! That hurt me so badly, back then. I'd get into fights consistently because of kids trying to make fun of her. But, after some time, I began to despise my mother, and I began to feel like she was an embarrassment to me.

I didn't want her to walk with me to school anymore, and I began not wanting to be in public with her. I stopped wanting to help her communicate with the "hearing."

As I reflect now, how sad was that! I can't imagine how my mother might have felt about me withdrawing from her in that way. Yes, I was only a child, and it seemed reasonable that it happened, but I wish I knew then what I know now. She deserved better! Adults have such an impact and make such an impression on young men and women. I believe all adults have a responsibility to be the best example for our children. You have an implicit obligation as an adult. Fulfill it!

At this point, I want to capture a period when I was about ten or eleven years old, the impact of which was to affect my future dramatically. My mother met a man named Russel. I'll never forget his name for very obvious reasons I'll talk about in just a moment. Russel and my mom were dating. I only realize that now, reflecting back, I remember him being around the house more often, until one day, my mom asked me a huge question. My mom asked me what I thought of Russel being my dad and them getting married. It seemed ok to me; from what I recall, I had no reason to say I didn't like the idea or that I didn't like him. He seemed to treat my mother and me well, and I didn't have any problem with him, or at least not one I could have remembered.

So, Russel ended up moving in, and they got married. Only a few short months had passed until he started being physically and verbally abusive to my mother. I remember one day, they were yelling and screaming at each other, and suddenly, my mother hit the floor in a loud horrible thud followed by a scream. I'll never forget that sound and seeing my mother lying there crying on the floor, and how afraid it made me feel! Well, that was only the beginning of what I came to realize was a horribly abusive relationship that my mother had with Russel. The abuse didn't stop with my mom, though. Russel started verbally and physically abusing me, as well. He would even have his friends hold me down so he could give me "knuckle sandwiches." What's a "knuckle sandwich," you ask? He would ball up his fist, poke out his middle knuckle, and bang his fist into my skull until he was tired of doing so, always leaving a few knots on my head to remind me of what an utterly abusive asshole he was.

As I'm writing this now, I wonder if he did the knots at the top of my head, intentionally, so no one could see the marks, the abuse, and the destruction he was inflicting on me. Russel was the very definition of an abusive father and husband. I remember, on another occasion, he and my mother were yelling at each other, and I was sitting on the couch watching and listening to them go at it. All of a sudden, he grabbed my mom and started hitting her, again and again, and again, so I ran to my bedroom and grabbed a baseball bat, ran back in the living room, cocked the bat as far back as I could, and swung it at that fucker's head, so hard it would have cracked his skull wide open. Fortunately, for my sake, I missed his head, but I hit his shoulder. He was definitely hurt and let my mom go to come after me. I immediately ran out of the house and didn't come back for a while.

No one should have to endure this abuse, but what was I, a young eleven or twelve-year-old David, to do? Of course, this "home environment" distanced me from my mother, my only "family." I would wonder why she let this man into our lives, let him disrupt what she and I had, why? I would cry out to God, "Why?" Is this really what "destiny" is all about?

My mother started drinking, drinking a lot. In fact, I would have to say she became an alcoholic. I guess it was her escape from the monster she let into our lives! She smoked and drank all day, every day, and would sit around singing gospel songs, smoking B&H cigarettes, and just drinking. I'm sure she didn't have a job and that we were on Welfare/Government Assistance. Our "family" quickly became the "typical" ghetto family on Welfare in the hood. I never wanted to be at home.

Why would I? I didn't want to deal with my drunken mother or my abusive stepfather. No, no way! I can remember going to the local liquor store to buy Budweiser beer and Benson and Hedges cigarettes for my mother, with a note from her authorizing the store to sell the items to me. We were definitely poor and living in the hood! We had food stamps and had to stand in line for government cheese. I don't know what happened; actually, I don't exactly know why. Why did we become that way? I can only blame it on my abusive stepfather, Russel!

Well, since my home life became an ultimate hell. I decided to start venturing outside of the house, more and more. I started hanging out with "the wrong crowd," guys who were selling drugs, gang bangers, and people who were always in some trouble. It was only "natural" that since we were in the hood, and I didn't want to be home, that I would gravitate towards a new "family." These were often older guys, "OGs," who were around the apartment complex and down the block. I befriended some of the younger kids my age that were well in between being a gang member or a gang affiliate. I started spending more time with the CRIPS and started smoking and drinking, just because they did. I didn't like either, but it was my new norm. I also started stealing from my mom, breaking into cars, smoking weed, and doing plenty of other things that an eleven-year-old kid shouldn't be doing. I had no "home," I just had the streets, my friends, my boys!

Young men and women often turn to the streets or drugs because of their home environment. Neglect, abuse, abandonment from a loved one is hard to deal with, especially at such a young and impressionable age. Having the "right"

7

mentors to mimic and the right surrounding are extremely important in the development of a young person.

Inevitably, I started committing crimes with my new found "family." I remember one morning, Rhino and Eddie, some of my "boys," and I decided not to go to school and go break into cars. Well, we would look for easy targets - cars with money or an easily accessible stereo or valuables left out in the open. We "smashed and grabbed" a few cars that morning and ended up with very little to show for all the efforts. And then, we happened upon a car that was parked in an apartment complex carport. We smashed the window and went to grab some stuff out of it, and right there and then, the owner came running down from his apartment, yelling and chasing us. We all ran, Rhino went one way, and Eddie and I went the other way. We lost the guy, eventually, but wow, that was close! On the way back to my house, we were on a rather major street, Baseline, on which there were situated a few car dealerships. "Look, it's Rhino!" said Eddie. Rhino was caught.

He was at one dealership together with the car owner whom we had just evaded. He was standing there with a police officer. We could see him and the cop inside because of the huge see-through glass windows at the dealership. Eddie and I tried to stay inconspicuous, and just as we were about to turn down a street, past the dealership, Rhino sees us, points us out, and in an instant, the cop comes running out of the dealership, heading to us. Eddie and I took off running, jumping over people's fences and through backyards. The situation resembled a chase scene from an action movie, and then out of the blue, a police officer comes out of nowhere. We're caught! He jumps out of his car, gun drawn, and we know that's it! As the officer orders us to place our hands on the police car, he grabs Eddie first. I think because he was bigger. And handcuffed him and started putting him in the back of the police car. Going through my mind is I don't want to go back to "kids" jail. I don't want the cop to catch me, and in that brief unguarded moment, I ran.

I ran as fast as I could again, over fences, through yards, and finally into an abandoned apartment complex. I hid there for a few hours; it seemed like forever. It had only been about three hours. I was hoping, the whole time, that Eddie and Rhino better not tell the police who I am and where I live. After several hours of just waiting, I carefully walked to my house, looking over my shoulder the entire time, wondering if the police were going to surround me, pull their weapons, and possibly shoot me just for being in the hood. As soon as I got to my apartment complex, out of nowhere, I got snatched up into midair, literally in the air, and slammed onto the ground, right in front of my house. It was the police officer from whom I had been running. He imminently started reading me my Maranda rights. I was busted! Wow, I couldn't believe it. Where was the "loyalty," the "code?" I mean, we were brothers, weren't we? I wasn't just mad; I was pissed the F-off. They betrayed me! I was so ready to "Get back at them!"

I got taken to the police station, fingerprinted, and then locked in a holding cell. After a few hours, another police officer put me into the back of another cop car and transported me to a juvenile detention center. All I could think of was, "Who ratted me out, who was it? They were going to get theirs." I had to go through the "routine." I had done it a few times before - get arrested, go to jail, get transferred to juvenile detention, wait for your court-appointed attorney to visit, have a hearing scheduled, see the Judge, and accept the "punishment." It seemed so easy, I guess. I don't remember how much "time" I did that time, but I think I was back out within a couple of months.

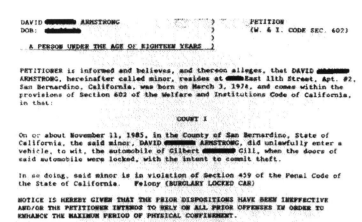

This wasn't my the first or last time I would find myself in handcuffs. My first arrest was when I was eleven years old for Felony Assault with a deadly weapon. I don't remember the incident but, I think I was trying to rob some lady for some money. As I think about it now, wow, this is ridiculous, and where was my "supervision?"

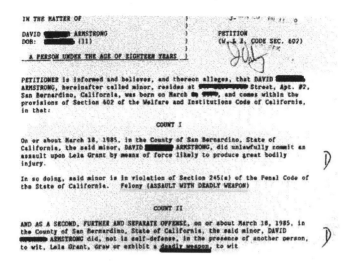

"I'm going to kill myself," haha, well, one thing I do remember about being locked up that time is never to say you're going to "kill yourself!" One day, while in juvenile detention, I was pissed off for some reason or the other, so I decided to say, "I want to die!" Well, that was a mistake. When you go on suicide watch in juvenile detention, it's no joke. They take everything away from you. I was stripped of all my belongings, no sheets, no shoes, just a gown, like a hospital gown, and that was it. I couldn't interact with the rest of the guys, so I had separate times from everyone else to come out of my room. It sucked! So, I quickly tried to get the psychologist to realize I wasn't serious.

When I got out of detention, I saw Eddie. He had gotten out before I did. Rhino said it was Eddie who ratted us both out, and I believed him. However, we weren't ever the same after that. Somewhere in the back of my mind, I felt like he told the police something about me too. He told me that Rhino was out of the neighborhood, and we never saw him again after that, lucky for him and us! Well, that was the beginning of many visits to the police station and juvenile detention.

I have so many thoughts, stories, examples of where things went wrong for me at such a young age. Where exactly was the turning point? How did things go from good to bad to horrible? All of this was beyond my control, like it was a cruel joke. It was like destiny for me to be born into this environment. I did not control my dad leaving, my mother marrying such a terrible person, or turning to the streets as a way out. It just happened! It was my destiny not to be "normal," I guess.

No One Wants To Be Poor…

Being poor sucks! Powdered milk, government cheese, ProWings (shoes for poor people), going to bed hungry. Sleeping with roaches was a daily thing, almost normal to a poor kid. Hearing gun shootouts outside the apartment was also "normal" and a nightly thing. No one wants to be poor. So, as a young adult/child, stay focused in life, and head towards the goal of never being poor again!

Back Home

I can't remember how long I had to stay in juvenile detention, but I remember my frequent trouble with the law becoming much more common. I had a court-appointed attorney, a social worker, and a judge all of a sudden. They all had good intentions for me; however, there's only so much the "system" allows someone in their positions to do. They would give me long talks, time in juvenile detention, and a lot of advice, but, ultimately, it was me that had to take action to change, but I didn't want to and didn't even know how to "change." I tried to keep from being around my house as much as possible. It was a hellhole there, and I'd rather be out in the hood than in the hell called my "home." The physical abuse only got worse and became more frequent. I guess no one noticed the bruises on me or the yelling and screaming that my mother and Russel did almost every night.

It was like a bad horror movie (the screaming, yelling, cussing, fighting, repeatedly) that I couldn't get out of and had to relive again and again. Enough! That was it! I was done with it. I just couldn't take it anymore! As Russel was beating my mother, I decided to step in and take control of the situation to end the abuse. I ran into their bedroom and grabbed his gun from his nightstand drawer. I wanted to kill him. I had to make the beating, the abuse, and the torture end! Well, he's still alive, and I'm glad because my life would look much different if I had killed him. I took his gun and pointed it at him, right at his head, and at the last minute, I lowered it and shot past him into the wall.

I guess it scared the shit out of him because he immediately called the police. Go figure! HE called the police, and they came and took me into custody... me! I pleaded with the police that I only tried to scare him so he would stop beating my mother, but that didn't matter. I was locked-up for a day or two and then on to see the judge. The same judge had seen me a few times when I had got into trouble before. The judge pronounced at that hearing that it was the last straw concerning his tolerance of me. That was it. They placed me in a boys camp in Pomona, California, after that incident. I was about twelve years old, and I was told that I'd be at the boys camp for a couple of years. It took me away from my friends and my mom and away from Russel and the abuse. The boys camp wasn't the best place. It was terrible, but in a much different way from being at home. It was much more tolerable. But, I was told what to do and when to do it, eat now, no snacks, walk now, run now, take these pills, etc. It was extremely strict at the boys camp, and we were under constant vigilance, 24/7. You couldn't do anything without being noticed. I wasn't used to that. It was opposite from my running the streets and coming and going, as I pleased.

The End

I earned the privilege to go home for the weekend, twice a month on a "home pass," provided that I was "good" during the previous week. One particular home pass weekend, I would never forget. I went home and did the usual things - spent time with my mom, hung out with my friends, watched TV - the regular thirteen-year-old types of things. The unusual thing about this particular weekend, at home, was that I had such a strong urge not to return on Sunday, as I was supposed to do and had always done. I would usually take the bus back to the boys camp on Sunday morning or afternoon, but this Sunday, I didn't want to leave. I wouldn't. I just couldn't bring myself to leave home for some reason. I made up excuses to tell my mother and step-father to stay - I missed the bus, or they'll come to get me tomorrow - any excuse just to stay. But this was a bit out of my character, a bit atypical for me to do.

I stayed an extra day or two because I wanted to spend it with my mom. I felt as though I couldn't leave her side. We talked and just hung out with each other over this self-imposed long weekend. I did not understand why or what compelled me to be so defiant and break the rules, knowing, full well, that the result would be that my weekend passes would be revoked. My getting into trouble was inevitable, but I did so, nonetheless. On either Monday or Tuesday, my social worker came and picked me up from my house. She lectured me on the whole forty-minute drive back to the boys camp, and, of course, I was "in trouble." They revoked my privilege to go on home passes. It

15

put me on restriction, and I ended up in a lot of trouble, of course, but I didn't seem actually to care.

I went on with my usual schedule with school and boys home life. Things were tense because of my weekend choices, but that was expected. Well, my decision to stay home was not in vain. Later that week or the following week, while sitting in class at school, I heard on the intercom, "Please send David Armstrong to the front office. He will be leaving for the day." What? Me? Why? What did I do this time? I went to the front office, and they told me someone would pick me up in just a few minutes by my social worker. I just knew I'd be taking a ride back to juvenile detention, but I couldn't figure out what for. What did I do this time! As my social worker walked up to the front doors, I could see this dim look on her face. She didn't look well at all. She told me we had to leave immediately.

As we drove, in silence, for a little while, she "let the cat out of the bag." She said, "David, your mom is in the hospital. She suffered a brain aneurysm, and she is in a coma. The doctors don't know how long she would last." Words I'd never forget. I felt blank, void of anything, like an incredible force was pulling me toward the ground like I was standing still, totally motionless while the world around me was moving twice the speed. What does that mean? Is she ok? What happened? Where is she? It was all I could scream, questioningly. I knew exactly what Deborah was saying, but I just didn't want to realize it or even accept it.

What was to follow was much more dramatic than the words Deborah had told me - my mother lying in a hospital bed, convulsing and shaking while she was in a seizure, her eyes rolling back in her head, nurses and doctors pushing Deborah and me out of the way as soon as I had walked into the room and doctors yelling "Get the kid out of here!" This picture of my mother is the last picture I have etched into my brain. I was only thirteen. This wasn't supposed to happen to me. It was so horrible! I ran out of the room and never saw my mom again. I was truly traumatized, in every sense of the word. I didn't want to believe that this was happening. No! I couldn't believe it. Deborah took me back to the boys camp, and all I really can remember is the feeling I had on the way back. It was like my soul was ripped outside of my body like I was watching all of this crap unfold in front of me and couldn't do anything about it.

My mother died shortly after that day in the hospital. Alone, void, abandoned, guilty, empty, and dead are accurate ways to describe how I felt. The one person I had was taken away from me. No matter if she was a "good" mom or "bad" mom, she was still my mother, and I loved her. Now I'm all alone!

To End It All

I couldn't stand going to my mother's funeral. It was so hard, too hard losing the one and only person, literally, that I had. I had so many emotions, so many feelings, so much to wish, worry, think, dream, and be terrified. What was to come? How will I live, survive, or even exist without the one and only person I had in my life? I had no father, no brothers, just one sister I hadn't seen since I was about seven years old. I had no family at all and now no mother. The one person I had in my life was taken away from me, but more than that, I felt as though she had abandoned me. Why me?

Without my mother, I became even more destructive, I just didn't care about myself, and I certainly didn't care about anyone else. I mean, why bother? What is there to live for if you have nothing and no one in life! I remember feeling so sad, so desperate, and so alone. One evening, I think a day or two, after my mother died, I decided to run away from the boys camp and end my life. I decided not to go to the boys camp "home" after school. Instead, I'd wander around the city aimlessly in the pouring rain. I was numb, just numb to life, and the world… to my very existence! I ended up under a bridge, shaking from the rain, cold, and from crying so much. I remember the pouring rain, like it was yesterday, pounding down so hard on my face as I cried uncontrollably.

I just wanted to know that things would be "ok," but I knew that would not be the case. Everything seemed so wrong. I felt so alone, not the same alone that you feel while you're falling asleep at night in a room by yourself, with no noise or distractions, not the alone you feel when you're out walking in a field, at night, by yourself and you look around, and all you see is field and stars, and you hear nothingness. No, this alone was different. The only way I can describe it was that my heart was empty and void, not just my physical surroundings, it was my soul! So, at that moment, under the bridge alone, I decided to end my life.

I grabbed a bottle that was close by, broke it open, and cut away at my wrists. I don't even remember it hurting; I just remember the blood. I cried and cut, cried and cut, until I couldn't do it anymore. Why won't I die? That's all I kept thinking, that's all I kept asking myself. Then I came to the realization, sadly, that I couldn't do anything right, including killing myself. So I got up and walked back to the boys home, bleeding and feeling even more unaccomplished and alone.

As I sit here, writing and looking at the scars on my wrist from that day, I realize I didn't want to die. I just wanted to be held. I just wanted someone to care about me and to tell me they had my back. I'm so glad that my life didn't end that day and that I've recovered and I've been able to help so many people in my life. And I'm glad, so glad, my experiences can help someone else not to hurt as much as I did.

Days of My Life

Being in the boys camp wasn't fun at all. And to make matters worse, since I tried to "deal" with losing my mother by attempting to commit suicide, they had me in therapy and on drugs. I hated the anti-depressants, or whatever they had me on. The drugs made me feel like I was having an "out of body" experience all day, all the time. I felt like a walking zombie (well, I don't know what a zombie would feel like, but I watch a lot of Walking Dead…LOL). Ok, let's get serious again.

I recall, one day, I was just so fed-up with taking these "zombie pills" that I decided to break into the closet and locker in which the medications were stored and take mine. I waited until everyone was asleep, snuck out of my room, crept down the hallway, and pried open the locker door where all the residents' medications were kept. No one heard me! I took only my pills. This would come back to haunt me! Then, I went to the bathroom, dumped all of my pills down the toilet, and went back to bed. Sometime later in the early morning, I had two staff members waking me up. They brought me to the common room and questioned me about the "break-in." Of course, I knew nothing! Well, it seemed very obvious to the staff who had broken into the locker since it was only *my* medication that was taken…hahaha. I had no clue. I wasn't owning up! Well, I decided to behave like a madman and started attacking staff, throwing furniture around the common room, and just acting wild and crazy. The staff members finally restrained me and took me to another house to "Sleep it off." Life was just so difficult. I was always angry at everyone around me, all the time, for no apparent reason. I felt as though I had no control over myself, my emotions, my anger, my sadness, or my feelings of loneliness.

My anger outbursts became more and more frequent, lashing out at everyone around me. One day, I was sitting in the cafeteria, and, out of nowhere, for no apparent reason that I can remember, I became furious and picked up my chair and throw it through the window. The window was one of these enormous glass windows, it must have been over twice my size, and I'm six feet tall. Bam! Glass all over the place, kids running away from me and the window, then here comes staff to restrain me again.

Another time, we were playing basketball, and one kid kept taking the ball from me. I'm not sure why I remember his name so well but, I do, Mario. I told Mario to stop stealing the ball from me, but he replied, "It's the game" or something like that. Well, he stole the ball from me again, and that was it. I ran as fast as I could and hit him as hard as I could in the back of his head. Thump! He goes down, and again, people come to restrain me. These temper tantrums, outbursts, and violent incidents were all too common in my life at the time. It became the norm for young Dave. It was like Groundhog Day, the same thing, day in and day out, and I guess the worse part is I just didn't care. You know when you do something for so long, it just becomes your new "normal," well, it was my new normal.

The Next Year

I still had another year left at the boys camp where I was located, and I often contemplated what was going to happen to me after I left. I knew that I had a sister, but she was much older than I, and she was already out of the house by the time I could remember. I hadn't seen my sister in several years and didn't know why she wasn't ever around.

I knew I had some uncles and aunts somewhere; we used to go to their house, and I remember playing with my sister (DelRose) in the pool. I have one memory of my uncles throwing me in the pool and not wearing any clothes, so I had someone else's shirt and my sister's socks on (all way too big for me). I have a memory of this photo, but I'm sure the photo doesn't exist at this point. Anyhow, the last time I had seen any of my family, I was probably about seven or thereabout. So, where was I going to live? What was going to happen to me once I left the boys camp? I mean, I would be literally homeless, no wait, I guess, I already was homeless. At fifteen, no child should have to ponder these things! But this was the life I was "given" my "destiny," and of course, I thought, why me?

Over the next year, I was in and out of trouble, but slowly, I started to "fit in" to my new life. I went to school but didn't do much homework or do much studying; I couldn't care less about my grades! I mean, what did they matter? I had much bigger problems to worry about in "life," so grades and going to college weren't even a thought in the back of my head.

Often, I had been "counseled" about my grades or my attendance, but I didn't care what the "adults" had to say. I mean, they didn't care; it was just their job to make me go to school and ensure that I study. If I did well, then it looked good on them. I have a distinct memory of feeling so alone in this world. For, if my mom and family could abandon me, why and how could anyone else care or love me.

Those of you who want to help. Understanding Love: See, when you haven't been loved or felt as though you haven't loved someone, it's next to impossible to "feel" as though anyone could love you in the future. I mean that the feeling most of us, "at-risk youth," have is that no one can love us since the people who were supposed to love us didn't. The experiences we've had to endure have left us empty and unable to truly appreciate love.

Are You Ready?

So, now it's time to leave the boys camp. My social worker had a conversation with me a few months prior. She told me she would try to find my family and that if she could not locate them or they didn't want to take custody of me, I would be placed in either a boys home, a foster home, or a group home. That meant that I would be spending my teens with no biological family and perhaps not even knowing who they were. Well, that's precisely what happened. Still, to this day, I don't know if she found my family or if she found them, and they said that they wanted nothing to do with me. What I know is that from that day, I was going to begin my journey bouncing around from home to home. Not that I had counted at all, but I've been in, let's just say, over a dozen group homes, foster homes, boys homes, and juvenile detention centers all over the San Bernardino and Los Angeles counties. I actually wouldn't be surprised if it were more like two dozen.

I've experienced all "types" of people managing these homes, ranging from individuals that legitimately cared about young persons, like me, in the homes, acting in a professional capacity, to those that only wanted the money for having children that are "wards of the state," in their homes. Of course, some work with children just because they need a job and a paycheck. Then, there are those who care and can actually connect and empathize with us, young men and women, who have more troubles than one could imagine. There are many people in the category of "caring" and "wanting," but they aren't able to connect or just haven't learned how to connect or how to make an impact in our lives. I've encountered plenty of people who wanted to help and wanted to make a profound impact on my life, but they just didn't know the right way to do so.

For example, telling someone that you care or want to see them succeed just isn't enough and isn't conceivable, sometimes. Each child you encounter is different and has had a unique experience with love. For me, the person who "loved" me or that was supposed to love me, protect me, and care about me allowed me to be abused, abused me herself, neglected me, and then abandoned me. Of course, it's not that simple, but it appears to be exactly that to a child or a young person. So, when someone told me that they cared for or loved me, I couldn't process that. I didn't know what the action of love meant. I knew about "being loved" wasn't something I enjoyed, so why would I want to be "loved" again. It makes little sense as I'm writing and thinking about this, but it's 100% the way many of us, youth in the system, feel.

How To "Connect"

There was a boy that decided he wanted to adopt and take care of a turtle. He had always loved everything about turtles and knew he would take care of his pet turtle very well. So, the first day after he finished petting and playing with his new friend, he grabs some meat leftover from the refrigerator and feeds the turtle. The boy goes to bed, and the next day, after school, he comes home, pets and plays with the turtle again, gives him another piece of meat from the refrigerator, and then goes to bed. Day three comes along; the boy goes to school, plays with his friend, grabs another piece of meat to feed the turtle, and goes to bed. The next morning, he notices his turtle had died from starvation. The turtle has eaten none of the meat. Turtles don't eat meat. You can have the best of intentions, but if the "action" is wrong. Just because you try doesn't mean you're trying the right way!

It's Hard to Be Loved When You Don't Know What Love is

Three people in my young life literally saved my life. The first was Sensei Otto Johnson, who was my martial arts instructor and a father figure to me. Sensei Otto was a psychologist at a boys home where I was placed, and he also worked at a mental hospital in the area. Sensei Otto was a massive man, 6ft 10in, and wide as a truck, hands that looked like they could uproot a tree right out of the ground. He was a professional martial artist and had competed worldwide. He looked like he could kill a man with just a thought… LOL.

Sensei Otto was just an amazing, loving, caring person, but I just didn't know that yet. Sensei Otto worked as a therapist at one of the boys homes where I was placed. And well, by his sheer size, he was noticeable, to say the least. Sensei Otto would conduct therapy sessions with the boys at the home, interact with them daily, and conduct a martial arts training session with the young men who were doing "well," those who were not getting into trouble and getting good grades in school, etc. I remember the first time I saw the boys in the backyard, doing this karate thing, punching and kicking the damn air, yelling, KIAI!!!!. "What the hell is this crap?" is what I thought.

Shortly after I got settled at the boys home, I decided that BIG BAD Dave was just going to run things and do what I wanted to do. I would come and go as I pleased, despite the house rules. Of course, I didn't care about grades or getting into trouble at school, and I was just in my own little world doing whatever I wanted to do. I knew the "game." If the group home staff called the police, the police may or may not find me, I might or might not spend the night in juvenile detention, and I may or may not go back to the same boys home, but I just didn't care at all! So, the "system" and its rules were just a game to me.

That is until, one evening, I decided to leave the house while Sensei Otto was there. He asked me where I thought I was going, and I told him, "out," and he said, "No, no, you're not! Go to your room, and you and I will talk." And of course, Big Bad Dave said, "Fuck off. I'll do what I want, and I'm leaving." Sensei Otto stood his 6ft 10in, over 300lbs self in front of the door, and said, "No, you're not leaving!" Well, I decided to push Sensei Otto. Why? I have no earthly clue. I sure the hell wasn't going to move his big ass, but there I was trying to push him out from in front of my path. I knew that staff couldn't touch us unless we "posed a threat to them or ourselves," so why I decided to put my hands on Sensei Otto is beyond me. I knew better. Well, he reached out and grabbed me by my neck, and not so kindly escorted me to my room.

I remember kicking and screaming, "I'm going to get my boys to kill you. You can't touch me. You're gonna die, my homies are gonna get ya ass," blah, blah, blah! Well, once I calmed down and started to think, of course, in the comfort of my bedroom, I didn't dare step outside of it. I thought about how Sensei Otto grabbed me, how he moved my body and how effortless it had been. Ok, he was much bigger and stronger than me, but it wasn't "strength" it was something else. His movements were so fast and seemed to just kind of flow. Was there some importance to this karate thing? The way he just handled me was crazy. He didn't even move, just bam, bam, and that was it. I thought to myself, "I want to be able to handle someone just like that." What if I learned this karate thing? I could beat anyone up. I already fought a lot and was good at it.

Once I calmed down and could think clearly, I decided to try to do this karate thing. But I had to earn the right to practice with the rest of the kids who were doing well. So, in just a few weeks or months, I showed a behavior change and asked if I could join. That moment changed my path, my future, my life, and my "destiny," forever. It led me to own successful martial arts schools, create a martial arts mentoring program for at-risk youth, teach abused women how to fight back mentally and physically, and help thousands of young men, young women, and parents.

I started training and enjoying the training sessions, but I would also try my newfound skills at school and in the street, now and then. I still had the "hood" in me and all around me, so it was hard to just "be good." But with Sensei Otto's guidance and encouragement. With his discipline and dedication to me, I slowly focused my energy entirely on martial arts. Martial arts started teaching me discipline, dedication, self-confidence, interacting with others, and working as a team with my fellow karatekas and other classmates.

We started training in judo and with weapons. I was competing all over California and even outside of the state, and I loved every experience I had! I would train every moment I had, every single day, and that paid off. I won several big martial arts tournaments, taught classes, and earned respect from my peers. This boosted my self-confidence and gave me a purpose in life other than just running the streets, selling dope, and breaking into people's cars.

"Purpose" in life is so important, and we don't always realize it. Without a sense of purpose, we get lost. We just let days turn into weeks, and weeks turn into months, months into years, and years into an entire life without a real purpose. It's a pity to have life and to waste it without purpose.

I had found a purpose in life that I truly began to love. Sensei Otto started letting me teach classes for him, and eventually, I was promoted to black belt after I turned eighteen. Martial arts and the dojo became my life and distracted me from the streets and my unfortunate reality. Sensei Otto was such a role model, an absentee father, and a person to whom I truly could look up. Until that point, I hadn't had a male role model to look up to or mimic my life afterward.

After I became an adult and started helping other at-risk youths, I realize that young men absolutely need a male to look up to and mentor them if their father isn't in the picture. It's extremely important for so many reasons. So, for you, young men out there, reading this book, it's your responsibility to find a male role model to help guide you, to help you along the path of life, to help you succeed. You can't and shouldn't try it alone. Believe me, I know! And if you are a successful male who's reading this book, you have a responsibility to help in any way you can. For sure, you now know that many young men need you, need your experience, your knowledge, and your love.

It Takes A Village

It wasn't only martial arts and Sensei Otto that helped me find a "purpose" in life. I had a couple of other mentors and people to whom I looked up that provided me with some guidance, mentoring, and purpose in my journey. We all should realize that there are plenty of moments in life we don't have control over, and the more we experience "life," the more we realize this or at least should realize it. A chance meeting, a split-second decision, turning left instead of right, speaking to that stranger or not, sometimes such a seemingly little thing can make a profound difference; it could mean life or death, success or being unsuccessful. We encounter these paths in life constantly, and what we choose during the encounter may determine the rest of your life.

The more you do, the more adventures you have, and the more people with whom you meet and surround yourself, the more chances of success and happiness you'll have. It's a simple numbers game. The more positive experiences you have and the more positive people you have in your life, the more positive "chance" moments of positivity you'll encounter. And the opposite also holds true. So, seek more opportunities for positivity, and they'll come. It is just a numbers game!

Ron Barnick, a Guardian ad Litem (GAL), a person who the court appoints to investigate what solutions would be in the best interests of a child, was appointed to be my GAL when I was about fifteen years old. He would take me out of the group home on little outings for lunch, dinner, ice cream, sporting events, etc. Ron was there to interact with me, almost like a big brother, friend, or substitute father. Then, he would give his report or assessment to the court and my social worker, providing details - what I want to do for my future, how my grades were, and if he thought the home in which I was currently placed was the right one for me things like that.

One time, they placed me in a boys home where a Blood gang member lived while I was a CRIP (a rival gang), and that was a tremendous problem. We would fight all the time, and, of course, we'd always be in "trouble," but this wasn't our fault. Why they would put us in the same boys home is beyond me. Maybe it was some huge plan by someone working for the state to solve gang violence, starting with us... hahaha.

One day, I remember this kid came into the bathroom while I was showering and pulling a gun on me. While I was actually showering... WTF! He snuck into the bathroom, closed the door behind him, and then ripped the shower curtain open and yelled, "Sup up now, Blood." I immediately lunged toward him, grabbing the gun. It turns out it wasn't even loaded, and it fell on the floor. I ended on top of him, naked... LOL, hitting him as hard as I could in his face. Of course, the staff busted in and took me off of him, him out of the bathroom, and let me get dressed to figure out what had happened. They removed him from the group home after that. Looking back on this, I can laugh but, I certainly didn't think it was funny at all at the time.

So, Ron nor I knew at the time that his role in my life would help shape it in such a dramatic way. Here's why I talk about the uncontrolled "chance" experiences in life. See, Ron was a pilot in the U.S. Air Force and a GAL volunteer to help inner-city youths. He flew a big aircraft, C141's, a cargo aircraft if I can remember correctly. Ron had flown all over the world, and he had things from all over the world in his house. When he invited me over to his place, I was always just mesmerized by all the "stuff" he had from all over the world. I would think, wow, the world is so big, and I want to see it. He had things from Italy, Germany, France, Thailand, Africa, I don't know, so many I really can't even remember now. But, I distinctly remember the feelings I had, the desire to see the world, travel, and hold and own things like Ron had. It was just amazing to me that there was a world outside of my hood and California. I'd look at all of these things from all around the world, and they made me feel like I could see from the places from where they came. What a feeling I had. It would be like I was dreaming. I'd ask Ron where he got each piece of memorabilia, if it had meaning when he went to that country, and how he got it. It was like an adventure to me, one that I could see myself being a part of it. I had such a deep desire to see the world!

Ron and I were completely different, absolutely nothing alike, he was an educated older white man, accomplished and certainly not from the hood, and I was completely opposite! But, I somehow connected with him, maybe through both of our desires to see and experience the world, maybe I could tell that he was a person who actually cared for me and my future, or maybe it was the fact that he would take me out of the group homes to attend events and dinners. I'm sure it was a combination of all. Ron was an amazing role model, an incredible mentor. Hell, I even considered him a friend. He was a very loving and kind person, and I surely needed that in my life. Because of Ron and his experiences in life, I somehow wanted to create my own experiences too. I not only talked to him about the world and what he'd seen but about his experience in the Air Force and about my possibly joining the Air Force too.

Ron unconsciously inspired me to want to join the Air Force and to see the world. See, if it weren't for Ron, I most likely would have never joined the Air Force and served for twenty-four years. I may not have even gotten out of the hood or done anything with my life. I give him a tremendous amount of credit for influencing me. But it was by chance all of that lined up to help me be the person I came to be. Again, many things in life are not always in our control, but we must take it and run with it when we see an opportunity. But even knowing what I wanted to do with my life wouldn't come without a challenge.

A Long Road

I still had a long road ahead of me before I could see the world. I first had to get through some phases - childhood, life, and graduate from high school. So, I had a couple of goals - to keep training and competing in martial arts and graduate high school, then join the Air Force. But the struggle of day-to-day life was real.

Growing up in group homes, foster homes, and boys homes is a tremendously difficult experience for most young men and women, myself included. You never felt settled, never felt stable, and never felt at "Home." When a person has their own space - house, apartment, hell, even if it's just a room - you could feel somewhat "at home," even if that space isn't the best environment or condition. But when you grow up in the "system" - juvenile detention, foster homes, and group homes - you never have a home.

I've lost count of how many placements - detention centers or homes - I had between ages twelve and eighteen. Still, it was definitely over a dozen, probably more like over two dozen. It's rather stressful for a kid to know that they might have to pack up and go to another house, another school, another entirely different environment. There were times I would arrive at a placement and not even unpack my little box of stuff and clothes because I knew I'd mess it all up and have to leave again. After a while, you become numb to it and not expect to leave the "home" but not even care. I just felt as though it was a "matter of time" before I'd be sleeping in another strange bed.

Apathy, Wow! Apathy is a horrible and dangerous mindset; it's worse than being or feeling negative. When you are apathetic, you don't care at all. It sets your mindset and emotions at zero. You get stuck in a very dark and lonely place and don't actually care. Another day is just another day. If you are working with anyone that seems apathetic, the one most significant thing you can do for him or her is to give them reasons to wake up, reasons to engage, and reasons to live.

Okay, back to moving my little "box of stuff," sometimes, people running the placements don't care about a kid's belongings. I remember losing so many things from placement to placement. Sometimes, your belongings (little box of stuff) will sit in your former room at the former boys home because you got moved from it suddenly. Sometimes people steal your stuff, and sometimes just in the process of moving things, they get lost. To this day, at the age of forty-six, I don't have a single photo of myself as a little kid. I can recall having a couple of baby photos of myself at some point, but they ended up missing from being transferred from one place to another. Things go missing when you go from "home" to "home," especially if you get transferred to juvenile detention. It is sad the number of my belongings that just went "missing." It is an unfortunate reality for most young men and women in the "system." I would have loved to write this book and reflect on photos of myself as a young kid, I'm sure it would have brought back some positive memories, but that's not the case. The oldest photo I have of myself is at around the age of fifteen, and I only have a few of those.

My advice to those who work with children, try your hardest to take care of their belongings, as you would your own or even better. Most likely, the photos or belongings are irreplaceable and will matter to them along their journey. You are their advocate, and they need you on their side.

Although almost everything is digital nowadays, social media keeps a lifelong history, if you let it. Back "in the day" you had to take a picture with a camera, use up the complete roll of film in it, take it to a place to develop the photos, wait a week or so unless you pay extra for 24-hour service, usually double the price. After all of that time and effort, you only have twenty-four pictures; oh, how times have changed!

The Long Road Continues

At that point, I had found some direction, some goal in my life, so I was trying to stay "good" and not get myself into trouble. By then, I was about sixteen or seventeen years old and kept on the path that had a light at the end of the tunnel. I had martial arts that occupied most of my time, I had Ron, who helped guide me and keep me on the right track, and I had a part-time job at Thrifty Foods/Drug Store, where I served ice cream. OMG, this job was so much fun, I could interact with people from my neighborhood, and well, of course, everyone got free ice cream or at least a big ass scoop of ice cream… LOL.

And then there was school. I don't remember a lot from school for some odd reason, but I do remember struggling with homework and having below-average grades—C's and an occasional B. Because I was forced to go to summer school, a Group Home rule, I had extra credits during the last year of high school, and I only had to take four classes, so I was out of school at lunchtime. After school, my daily program was going to work, going to karate practice in the evening, and going back to the boys home at night for dinner, and then studying if I needed to. This sort of full daily schedule was a perfect thing for me because it kept me busy and lacked time to get into trouble.

Those of us working with young men and women try to engage with them to figure out what they are interested in and the things they like or would like to do. Get them involved and fill their days with their interests. Not only will you help them stay out of trouble and away from the "friends" who encourage negative behavior, but you'll also help them find the things they enjoy and perhaps something that will become a lifelong "thing" for them, possibly even a profession. Finding our interests early on and becoming good no, great at those interests is truly part of "What life is all about."

So, there I was, seventeen years old, and finally, for the first time in my life, I'm "on the right track" but, this is not without some severe bumps in the road, before and after "getting straight." One doesn't just learn a new behavior, a new different way to be or want to be, and suddenly just delete every learned behavior one has had, every memory, and every experience. That's not the way life works. I had to remold, to remodel myself into the person I now wanted to be in life, and that only happens with a lot of effort and dedication to stay on the right path that I set for myself.

I still had a temper and anger management problem, a severe one, actually. I would fight, just because I knew how, and felt like people were "disrespecting" me often. There were times I would start a fight with a random person who was just walking by me. I'd say, "Sup Cuz, what the fuck you lookin' at." The response would often be "Nothing, man," but it didn't matter what his response would be. The fight or ass-kicking was already started, and he just didn't know. I had so much hurt and anger inside, even though I could see the light at the end of the tunnel, even though I was trying to "be good" and become the person I knew I had deep inside. It was hard... very hard. I had been through so much. It's a lot to deal with - being so alone, abandoned, abused, watching your only parent die, changing so many homes and environments, not knowing what love or even like, as an emotional state, really is. It was a lot to overcome and change but, even though I had Sensei Otto, Ron Barnick, some psychologists and social workers trying to help, the real "help" had to come from within first.

My Last "Home"

So, Richard Crew and I were best friends in high school. We were inseparable! We were the school "crushes," we were "bad boys," and we got into a lot of trouble together. See, Richard and I had one huge thing in common. We both liked to fight, so we would start fights. I know that it may be strange to some of you to picture teens just starting random fights, but this is typical in the "hood." You were either prey or predator, the end! Anyway, besides fighting, we would break-dance together. We even would come up with routines to perform at school or parties. It made us even more popular in the neighborhood and at school. Richard and I were and still are, big boys, so two big guys running around starting fights and breakdancing in the hood was a bit atypical. Wow, thinking back now, I remember that we had these business cards printed up that said "Gunz and Ammo" with a bicep flexing. We would give them to girls at the mall all the time... Hahaha, too funny! Richard and I did everything together for about a year, and I got to know his family very well. The group home I was staying in was down the street from his parent's house, and Richard's parents got to know me and liked me a lot. I'd spend a lot of time with Richard's family - holidays, dinners, even one Christmas.

One day Richard's father, Richard Sr. and his mother asked me to sit and talk to them for a bit. They said they knew what kind of boys home that I resided at and that it wasn't the best environment. They also said they loved me as a son, and well, wanted to know if they could make it work, would I want to come to live with them. It shocked me. I mean, really me? I was still a bad kid, not as bad as a few years before, but I still had tremendous issues - getting into fights, suspensions, low grades, and coming and going as I pleased. But it also struck me with a feeling of acceptance, love, and caring. These things I didn't really know from a "family." I mean, I had Sensei Otto, who was like a stern father figure who would discipline me in the dojo, the martial arts school, and I also had Ron, who was like a surrogate mom, in a good way, to me.

He was more nurturing and caring toward me than Sensei Otto. But, I never had a "family" - a mother and father who cared about me - to guide me, talk to me, and keep me in line when I needed it. Anyhow, I was thrilled for a few reasons, I'd have a "home," and I'd also be leaving the "system."

Richard's parents started the process of getting custody of me, even though my social worker tried to talk them out of doing so. She told them I was in horrible shape, a lot of trouble and a lot of work. Richard Sr. also decided to open a foster home for kids. I can't exactly remember how long it took for the "process" of getting me moved from the boys home to Richard's family's house. Still, from what I remember, it didn't take long before I could move and hopefully start a new chapter in my life. I remember my social worker telling me that everything was approved to move to Richard's place. I was ecstatic to be leaving the "system," somewhat. I'd still be a ward of the state, but no more shuffling around from boys home to boys home and in and out of juvenile detention. I'd have a "stable" place, or so I thought.

Home is Home

So, after I settled into Richard's place, I noticed things were different from when I was just coming over to hang out. Not different, like having chores with some rules and discipline, I expected that. They expected me to do certain things like pray to God, go to church, not curse, be home for dinner, and have good grades in school. These rules were a bit different and new to me, and I couldn't say that I liked them at all. But it kept me occupied and relatively out of trouble.

At that point in my life, I was around sixteen or seventeen years old, and I was trying to get out of the hood and do something with my life. I knew that I was a driven type of person who liked to lead, so I'd either be a gang leader or do something positive in my life. So, every day, I was trying, but it was difficult, while you were in the negative environment, being influenced, to fall back into the "norm." So, I would slip and slide back and forth between trying to be "good" and doing "bad," and it was so easy to fall back into what was expected, into what was expected for you, in the hood. I spent around a year trying martial arts, football, work, hanging out with friends, and seeing Ron and Sensei Otto.

Practice Makes Perfect

My plate was rather filled when I was around seventeen. Not only did I have school and was able to maintain decent grades, enough to graduate... LOL. I also was working at a new job that I bulldozed my way into (I'll explain in a sec). I was playing football and training/teaching/competing in martial arts. Martial arts was my life! I would train almost every day for hours. I was the first one in and the last one out of the dojo, almost every day, and I loved it. Before and after class, I would clean the school, and I'd train by myself for hours, and if I could have, I would have lived in the gym. I just loved it. I was finally good. I mean, really good at something in my life. School was alright, I was fighting much less, and my grades were pretty good, oh and there was my new job.

So, here's the "I'll explain in a sec" (a little story); On my way to school, I would see this little "race car." It was a Nissan 240Z, and there was a 'for sale' sign on it. I would pass by it every day and think, man, I want this car! But, I couldn't afford it, and hell, I didn't even have a driver's license. Despite all of that, I wanted it, and I wanted it badly. One day, I knocked on the guy's door and asked him if I could buy it...with a "catch." I didn't have all the money for it. He thought it was cute or admirable, so he said he would let me make payments on it until I paid it off. I don't remember how much it was, but I remember it took me a few months to finish paying it off.

I would get my check, cash it and put half, if not more, on the car, which lasted for months. I was so determined to have that car. And well, I did everything it took to have it. So, finally, one day, it was all paid off, and he handed me the keys and the pink slip. I was ecstatic about my first car! But, I still had one problem, I didn't have a driver's license, and because I was still a "ward of the state," I couldn't get one until I was eighteen. Of course, this didn't stop me from driving my new car, not even a little…LOL.

Oh, and I bulldozed my way into a new job. So, again, there was an elementary school on the way to school that I would pass by. Somehow, I knew that they had an after-school program for the elementary kids. I stopped inside to ask if they were hiring. I'm not sure if they had something posted somewhere or someone told me about the position, but I stopped and asked. I got the standard answer - fill out a job app, and we'll contact you. So, I did just that. I filled out the application, right then and there, and gave it to them. And then I proceeded to stop by there every day. I would ask if they had taken a look at my application and had filled the position yet. Barbra Horzen was the director there for the after-school program, and she knew my name very well. It must have been almost every day for a month or so until she finally gave in and gave me a job…LOL.

She must have gotten tired of seeing me or knew that I was a determined and passionate person who did not accept no for an answer. Yep, I think it was that! I've never been the type of person who accepts "no," as a matter of fact, that's when the challenge begins. You say no, and I say challenge accepted. So, I got the job. It paid well, and I enjoyed working with kids. Barbra and I are friends to this day, and I tell her how much I appreciated her giving me the job and being so nice to me. She made an enormous difference in my life and is a part of my success and the person I've become today. And I tell her that, so she knows how much that means to me. Barbra later started working with the juvenile system as a foster parent. She actually still is a foster mother to this day and has mentored and helped hundreds of young men and women. Bless her, what an amazing woman!

So, besides a good job that I enjoyed, Sensei Otto also had me teaching his children's karate class, and I was good at it. The kids loved me, and I enjoyed teaching them. I was also competing, a lot, in martial arts tournaments and winning, winning big, too. The school and Sensei Otto traveled all around California, Nevada, Utah, and Texas to compete in tournaments, and it was so amazing! The competition and discipline of martial arts were precisely what I needed in my life. Almost every weekend, we had a tournament to attend and compete in, and I would win my division almost every time. For the first time in my life, I remember feeling that I was good at something. Good enough to win, teach, and to be admired. It was a fantastic feeling and has shaped me into the person I am today. At the time, I had no clue that the dedication I had to martial arts would lead to my being able to do so much good for so many people, young and old. Being able to own several martial arts schools and influence so many people, young and old, is just a fantastic feeling!

It's allowed me to own my martial arts mentoring program for at-risk youth, become the VP for the Board of Directors for a non-profit that has helped thousands of young men in the "system," as well as mentor so many people, young and old, in my own martial arts schools. But we'll get more specific about that later on in the book. I was finally doing "good," but it wouldn't last too long.

Giving a child something to be passionate about and interested in is a tremendous deal. So many of us are just forgotten. We don't have anyone pushing us to do extracurricular activities, exploit our talents, or even find what that we are talented or passionate about something. It's a shame that so many children go through their childhood and end up later in their lives, not knowing what their potential could be or would have been. If only they had just the right amount of encouragement and the right person in their corner, and you're out.

Many people don't know this, but when you have no family on which to rely. You are in the "system" - juvenile detention, boys homes, group homes, foster homes - you don't have a "Plan B," hell, you don't even have a "Plan A." What I mean is there's no fallback, no cushion, no option, once you turn eighteen and graduate high school. I graduated from high school, and I was homeless. That's it! We get kicked out of the house with no place to go. It doesn't matter if you were doing well or if you were going to college. Nothing matters; you are homeless. No one gives you $10,000 to start your life, and colleges don't just let you attend for free, with room and board. So, where are we supposed to go, what are we supposed to do? I'm not the exception. I'm the rule. Many young men and women in the "system" don't have opportunities after graduating high school. We're thrown out to the wolves. The United States has the highest conviction and recidivism rate globally, and we want to ask ourselves why. One major contributor to this is that we are not setting our youth up for success. It's quite the opposite; failure is the destiny of many of us.

I was so shocked and saddened that, once Richard Sr. stopped receiving money from the state for me, he expected me to go. To this day, I still don't understand why and how he could have expected me to get out of his house, but that was the expectation. He laid the news on me a bit after I graduated. I didn't have much of a plan for what I would do after graduation. I knew I wanted to continue to teach martial arts, and I also was toying with the idea of joining the Air Force, like Ron. I was also good at football, so I thought of trying for a scholarship to play football at UCLA or USC. So, since I needed to find a place to live, and honestly, I wanted nothing to do with Richard Sr. anymore, I asked my girlfriend, at the time, if I could ask her parents to live in one of the abandoned campers in the field, in the back of her house. They had a vast field, probably two or three acres, and many abandoned cars, junk, and campers. I reckoned maybe I could fix up one of the campers and make it into a decent place to live until I figured out what I was going to do with my life. I asked my girlfriend's parents, and they agreed, I think a bit reluctantly, but a yes is what I got.

So, I spent a weekend cleaning the camper out, and the next weekend moving what little worldly possessions I had into the camper. It wasn't all that bad. I mean, it wasn't like living in a house with heat, air conditioning, or someplace to cook and eat, but I also wasn't sleeping on the street, so I was grateful. Plus, my girlfriend's parents were amazing to me.

Her dad was a mechanic and would show me how to fix my car all the time. I learned how to replace brakes, change oil, fix a carburetor, and even replace a head gasket in my car (you know, the one I mentioned above, the Nissan 240Z that I worked so hard for), which would have been difficult and expensive, otherwise. I'll always be grateful for the compassion, kindness, love, and skills her parents showed me.

Also, staying there afforded me some time to think about my future. I was destined to be a product of my environment. I mean, most of us are. The truth is, the majority of us who are born into the ghetto, the hood, the trailer park, and the projects never leave. For many, our kids, their kids, and generations, before and after, stay in the environment they were born into like they were destined to be there. I always felt as though I had something more significant to accomplish, something beyond my written destiny. The problem is, I had a fork in the road in front of me. I could stay, sell drugs, be a big-time drug dealer, or take a chance on leaving and not knowing what I was going to "be." I even had thoughts of being a hit-man, a contract killer. It seems crazy, but honestly, I wanted to do that. I mean, I wasn't afraid of anything, I had nothing to lose, and further, I was a "martial artist." So, why not?

Well, obviously, I didn't end up taking the easy and more "natural feeling" fork in the road.

The Air Force

I decided to take the "road less traveled" and joined the Air Force. But, even attempting that wouldn't come without a challenge. I had to take a test called the Armed Services Vocational Aptitude Battery (ASVAB). The ASVAB "Scores you in four critical areas - Arithmetic Reasoning, Word Knowledge, Paragraph Comprehension, and Mathematics Knowledge. All count towards your Armed Forces Qualifying Test (AFQT) score. The AFQT score determines whether you're qualified to enlist in the U.S. military. Your scores in the other areas of the ASVAB will determine how qualified you are for certain military occupational specialties and enlistment bonuses. A high score will improve your chances of getting the specialty job and signing the bonus you want. Scoring high on the ASVAB will require study and concentration. Don't skimp on preparing for this test. It's your future. Get the most out of it." *The definition is taken from* <u>military.com</u>

My first attempt at taking the ASVAB was an utter failure. I didn't score high enough even to be considered by the Air Force. The Air Force has the highest baseline score requirement, and even though the Army, Navy, and Marines would accept me, the jobs they were offering weren't what I wanted to do. Plus, I really wanted to join the Air Force.

After speaking with the Air Force recruiter, he told me to buy or check out from the library, ASVAB study guide books, study hard, and retake the exams. One catch, I had to wait for six months before I could retake the ASVAB. So, I was told to go live in a trailer in the back of my girlfriend's parents' house with no money, and oh, my car was broken again. The Army and Navy recruiters were calling me and inviting me to functions all the time. I began considering the Army since I didn't want to keep staying in the trailer. The Army recruiter kept inviting me, so, while considering, I decided to go ahead and attend one of their functions.

It was some banquet type of deal, with other potential recruits and a bunch of current Army personnel. It was a standard type of deal, from what I remember, until two guys came out on stage, one much older than the other. The older guy started barking orders, counting, all "military-like" pushups… bark… bark… bark… one, two, three… bark… bark… bark. You get the idea. Well, this was a big no for me. I understood that I'd have to "listen" and that the military was disciplined, but this was a bit over the top for me. So that was it. I had to wait for six months until I could retake the ASVAB. I went to my local library and checked out two ASVAB study guides, and that was my life. Every day for hours, I would study and practice; even my conversations with friends and my girlfriend were test-prep questions…LOL.

In the meantime, I had to earn some money legally. I knew if I got caught selling drugs, I'd be in adult jail and could not join the Air Force, so I started working Heating Ventilation & Air Conditioning (HVAC). OMG, it was a tough job! My back, neck, and entire body hurt every day after working ten plus hours. There were plenty of days that I just wanted to quit and do something much easier, like sell some weed, but I knew what that meant. I had given up and didn't want to sacrifice for my goal. I couldn't bring myself to give up. It wasn't in my nature; it wasn't "me," so I kept working, kept studying, and waited the six months to retest. The wait was hard. It was difficult to resist temptation, easy money, smoking weed, and being around friends, but it was a sacrifice that I knew I had to make. It was an absolute necessity to accomplish a bigger goal, a sacrifice for a dream to break my destiny.

David M. Armstrong

After the Wait

The six months went by, and I retook the ASVAB test. The test was difficult, but I knew many of the answers, as opposed to the first time I tested. After a few weeks, my Air Force recruiter called me and gave me some amazing news. I had passed and would be accepted into the Air Force if I pass the physical and mental exams, including a drug test. I wasn't anxious about passing either, for I had kept away from drugs for months and well, mentally…that's a whole other story… LOL.

Finally, I had a date to in-process the Military Entrance Processing Station (MEPS) in Los Angeles, and I was super excited to go. I remember my in-processing date was in February. I remember it was in February because of two huge reasons: my birthday on March 3rd, and I was in basic training during my birthday. The second "huge" reason was MEPS in Los Angeles burned down a few months before I was supposed to go, and I had to in-process in San Diego instead of Los Angeles. The LA MEPS burned down during the Rodney King Riots. It was crazy in LA, fires everywhere, sirens going for hours, buildings burning down…just crazy!

I hopped on a bus and went to San Diego to in-process and started my new life. I was nervous, the entire bus ride over, thinking about what to expect. I stayed in a hotel with another guy who was in-processing, and if memory serves me right, he was going into the Navy. The next day, someone came to collect us and take us to MEPS. In-processing was a series of physical tests, a physical medical exam and then a "sit down" with a guy who kept telling me he knew I smoked weed and that I have to tell him, right then and there... LOL. He didn't scare me!

So, I got through the exams, and then, before I knew it, I was flying to Texas for Air Force basic training. My recruiter and Ron had told me what to expect at basic training, so nothing came as a surprise, except I made Dorm Chief halfway through the basic training. Dorm Chief was a position where one recruit was in charge of the group of recruits, a leadership position.

He or she reports to the Training Instructor (TI), the person in charge, who has been in the military for a little while and gave direction to the dorm recruits. It was so cool that someone recognized my leadership abilities, but then I was quickly demoted. I just had to laugh to myself. I think around week three or four, the TI had said something that I laughed at while we were all lined up, and of course, I didn't laugh on purpose, for he certainly didn't mean to be funny. But I was always playful and full of jokes, so laughing didn't surprise me at all... hahaha. After being demoted, I continued with basic training and did well with all the exams and physical tests. Of course, it was a big "head game." They tried to break you, all to get through to the mentally weak recruits and end up with the more "suitable" recruits. It was a challenging eight weeks, but I got through it with ease.

The News

So, I spent my birthday at basic training and got some massive news from my wife. Oh yeah, I got married, but more on that in just a sec. So, the "huge" news was I was going to be a dad!!! Yep, me...a father! It was good news... we were trying to have a kid. Not sure why. I guess it was "the normal thing" and so was getting married. Oh, yeah, my first marriage. So, I ended up marrying the girl I was dating at the end of high school, the girl that convinced her parents to let me stay in the trailer in the field in the back of their house. I have no idea how I ended up getting married to her and having kids. I mean, it just kind of happened on purpose. What I mean by that is, I'm living "with" her and getting close to her family, and then, suddenly, her aunt came up to us and said, "We need to talk." Her aunt was very religious and kind of forced us and expected us to go to church all the time. So, her aunt said, "I had a dream with you both in it last night, and you both died," WTF!

"You both are living in sin and need to be married ASAP, or else this dream will come true... Jesus says so," again... WTF. That scared the crap out of me. What scared me even more, was a week after that, I lost my job doing HVAC. He went out of business, and then my ex and I got into a big car accident that totaled my car, my precious 240Z, that I had worked for so hard. Her aunt said, "I told you so, and things would get worse if you are living in sin," so I was like, oh crap, ok, let's do it. Her aunt paid for the wedding, and well, that was that... I'm married.

It also made sense since we were in a "relationship," if you can call it that when you're seventeen and eighteen years old... LOL and that I would be going away from California after I graduated from basic training. The next "normal" thing to do was to have a kid; yeah, I know. I would never give this advice to an eighteen-year-old, but it worked out for me.

So, I'm at basic training, married, and now about to be a father and graduate from basic training and go to Security Forces school at Lackland Air Force Base, Texas. I was so excited to start a real-life, a family, a career, and see one more state. Texas, here I come!

Am I Ok?

So, I graduated from basic training as well as technical training, but not without an issue. While at Security Forces training, my knee started hurting. One day, I saw the doctor. They did some tests and a few days later told me I had Patellar Femoral Syndrome, "I have what?" My knee wasn't correctly aligned, and it caused my patellar tendon, the tendon that is attached to your kneecap, to become inflamed and hurt a lot. Anyhow, the real problem is that they told me I couldn't be in the Security Forces. What! Why! Really! That was my dream. That was exactly what I joined the Air Force to do. Why is, once again, my dream being ripped away from me? It seems like everything I try to do just doesn't work out for me. Why me?

Well, I didn't know it at the time but, it would be a "blessing in disguise" for me to be forced to change jobs. So, I got called into someone's office, and he said, "Armstrong, you are not qualified to be in the Security Forces career field because of your knee condition. You are going to have to make a decision. You can either leave the Air Force or find a different job that you are qualified for." All I wanted to do is join the Air Force and be a Security Forces Officer, and now, just because of my stupid knee, I can't. I wished I would have never complained about my knee, but we were doing so much running, in boots, hiking, etc. It just was hurting so badly.

Ok, what jobs could I choose? So, this guy started giving me a list of jobs I could go into, and this "computer" thing seemed interesting. So, I said, ok, let's do that! Well, that began a twenty-four-year career in the Air Force that I have never regretted once.

"You can take the Homeboy out of the Hood, but not the Hood out of the Homeboy." Many of us don't realize that we are a product of our environment and that changing the "product" is a complicated process. I've worked with many people who work with youth and sometimes don't realize that people don't change overnight. Most of the time, change has to be a very deliberate process that takes plenty of time. So, if you are working with at-risk youth, understand that they can and will change their learned behavior, but it will take time and effort from you and them.

I'm All Better…Right?

So, now that I had accomplished my dream of joining the Air Force, I'm married, I have a son, so what's next? Life is good, right? Well, no, not really. Although I have undeniably made progress in life and have worked hard to accomplish some of my dreams and goals, I hadn't worked on who I am, and some learned and instilled behaviors and mindsets I possessed. I still had a terrible temper, I still couldn't read or write very well, I definitely had an attitude, and the Air Force would not tolerate any of that. I received reprimands and counseling and was sent to remedial reading and writing courses and sent to Mental Health to talk to a psychologist. I still had a lot of work and growing to do, but the problem was that I didn't know it at the time. I was only twenty years old; what does a twenty-year-old kid from the hood who grew up with no parents or proper guidance know? I sometimes felt as though the world was against me - my supervisors, commanders, friends, acquaintances, and even my wife. They all were against Dave. That's what I believed.

Of course, that was far from the truth, but what is "the truth?" I think in life, there are **three** truths: "**your** truth," "**other people's** truth," and "**the** truth." One "truth" doesn't necessarily trump the other "truth." "your truth" matters to you. It's your perception of the circumstances, and whether or not it's "the truth," it still affects you, your judgment, and your attitude. So, "my" truth was that everyone was against me, I had had to fight all of my life, and well, I would have to continue to fight because nothing would come to Dave easily. Although there was some "truth" to that, it wasn't "the truth." The truth is the Air Force needed me to do my job efficiently, and if I couldn't read or write and walked around with an attitude, well, I couldn't do my job. My supervisors and commanders, most likely, cared about me just as much as they did about the Air Force's mission and they needed and wanted me not only to be able to read and write but, they needed me to lose my negative and combative attitude. Everything came full circle. After supervising and leading hundreds, if not thousands of Airmen and people, I realized that there's a necessary balance between people's personalities and productivity. I've experienced thousands of personalities, and everyone is different; everyone has his or her own "thing," and that's ok. Each person must understand that sometimes their baggage doesn't belong at work and needs to be left at home.

Understanding that there are three "truths" in life can be an absolute lifesaver. Suppose you can realize that everyone is just a product of their environment, coupled with who they are today. In that case, you'd realize that people can see the same thing/ occurrence/ person/ situation entirely differently. Why, because each person's perception is based upon what they've experienced throughout their lives, not yours.

Look, Mom, I've Made It!

I don't just "owe it to myself" or Sensei Otto or Ron Barnick; I also owe a huge part of my success to the Air Force and the Supervisors I had, the Commanders I worked for as well as my peers and my Air Force friends. The Air Force taught me so much! Not just about myself or interacting with others, the Air Force was the family that I never had and desperately needed.

We all need some training, molding, family - maybe it's not your biological family - to help you through this thing called life but having a "family," a community, even just a friend or two. Hell, even a mentor or life coach, just someone who sees you as important. Through excellent role models in the Air Force, they shaped me into a proper Airman, a productive member of society, and an overall good person. But, as with any and everything in life, "you can always be better," and well, I had plenty of "baggage" that was following me, like my bad temper. My temper would get me into trouble, but mostly my temper came out with my wife. We would fight, like a literal fight, scream, yell, throw things, etc. That was the norm and happened regularly. The anger management classes helped, but they didn't extinguish the behavior altogether but impacted the REST of my life.

I remember one day, my ex and I were fighting about something, doing the usual, yelling, cussing, pushing, and throwing things, and suddenly, I snapped and grabbed her and threw her across the entire living room. I'm a pretty big guy - 6ft, 225lbs with a lot of muscle - and my wife was far from being close to my size. I remember her hitting the wall with a huge thud! I left the house, and about an hour later, I came back only to find the police waiting for me. Of course, I didn't tell them the truth. I told them we argued and that I left. She didn't have any bruises or anything but, the police said they had to arrest me. I couldn't believe it. I thought my days of being in handcuffs were over! I was confused, angry, embarrassed, and disappointed in myself. I never wanted to lose my temper like that again, but it happened. I never wanted to hurt her, but it happened. I never wanted to be handcuffed and arrested, but yeah, it happened.

What now? Well, the judge ordered me to (you guessed it) Anger Management Classes, in addition to Marriage and Family Therapy. After some time in both, I started to "get it" I learned that getting angry and losing control was a choice and that I could choose to respond to a trigger in any way I wanted to respond. Slowly but surely, I got better at controlling my temper and realizing I had a choice in how I would respond to things or people.

You are a product of your environment, and your anger outbursts, violent temper, and response to triggers - what people do or say to you - are all learned behaviors. You can choose to develop the skills and abilities to overcome your learned behaviors, and in time you will have complete control of yourself. But it takes work and commitment to yourself as well as a good mentor or role model in your corner. Don't be afraid to seek help, to find the right person, or to join a group to make yourself better. You owe it to yourself and your future to overcome your limitations.

The Air Force - The Gift That Keeps on Giving

As I reflect on myself and my current personality, I can see how much of the Air Force is in me. It is part of who I am at my core. The forty-six-year-old Dave is disciplined, determined, and I have integrity in all that I do. I serve before I think of myself. The Air Force's core values are integrity first, service before self, and excellence in all we do. It instills these values in us, and anyone that lasts as long as I did, twenty-four years, has these core values ingrained as part of his/her soul. Throughout the twenty-four years, it has given me the ability to lead and follow, learn and grow, and help mold and shape others. The Air Force's structure of growing leaders - real leaders with the skills and abilities to lead - and help develop others is fantastic. I have worked in such incredible locations and for absolutely amazing people. I've gone from a joint military assignment in Hawaii to working directly for a two-star General, to working inside of a granite mountain, Cheyenne Mountain (NORAD), Colorado, to being a Wing Inspector General for Lajes AFB in the Azores, Portugal.

And not to forget my life-changing assignment in Greece, where not only was the position and job fantastic, but I met my amazing wife and fell so deeply in love with not only Vasiliki but with the country. So much so, I decided to retire here!

The things you do, who and what surrounds you, shape you. They mold you for negative or positive, for good or bad,

so that you ultimately possess the skills and ability for success in life or not. So, pay attention to what's around you and what you are absorbing into your soul, it matters, and your life depends on it!

The Air Force...Trip

I really can't say enough positive things about my twenty-four years in the Air Force. As a young airman, I did "Young Airman Things," and looking back at it; I know that I was a bit above average and showed a lot. I always had an innate drive, that internal drive to be the best to lead and to set the standard. I requested some of my juvenile court records a few years ago, and to my surprise, there was a report from one of my teachers from when I was in the second grade. It's SO strange that features of how and who we become could have been identified when we were so young. I'll share what she wrote:

1982/1983, Grade 2

<u>Under Interests, Activities, Leadership:</u> "David seems to enjoy school when he's here–likes all activities and is a leader, but sometimes leads in the wrong direction."

<u>Under, Family and home relationships out of school responsibilities</u>: "Parents have not attended conferences."

<u>Under Attitudes and feelings about self, peers, and school:</u> "David is easily offended when he considers that he is affronted by other students–reacts physically. Can be verbally abusive to others."

The Air Force facilitated this innate fire I had to lead and succeed. I remember one of my court-appointed special advocates (CASA), much like Ron Barnick, acknowledged that to me. He said that he "Can see that I have the natural ability to influence people and to lead, but where you lead people to and what type of people you lead is entirely up to you." Frank, my CASA, took me to a prison and a college and emphasized that I would be successful at it no matter what I do. Where I was to be successful was up to me and my actions NOW—what a profound statement. I had an obvious choice, but what wasn't clear then is what choice I would make.

Through the Air Force, I was able to do so much, to grow tremendously, and I just can't say how much I'm thankful for what the Air Force has done for little Dave. Not only have I been able to attend college, but I've also attended fantastic leadership courses, I've been able to learn from some of the most amazing people, and I've been taught how to be a leader by some of the best leaders in the Air Force. I don't want to give too much about my Air Force career away because that's going to be my second book, "The Air Force Saved My Life" but, I can say that it has been a prosperous career with a lot of ups and downs but, way more ups. Awards and opportunities presented themselves at every step. Speaking of awards, I've won many but, the nearest and dearest one was winning the Military Outstanding Volunteer Service Medal twice! Throughout my career, I've continued to give back to people. I truly believe that connecting with people that may need help or are less fortunate is essential, and it's helped mold me into who I am today.

You Don't Control Your Destiny… Do You?

I often say that we have no choice of where we were born, what complexion or nationality we are, who our parents are, or our life's social environment; we're just born, and boom, that's it, and everything else just is. So, I had no choice that my environment would be what it was, and I had no choice if my mother was going to marry an abusive man, that she would become a drunk and then die, leaving me abandoned, all alone for the rest of my youth. Those choices were not mine, but I did have choices along the way. What was I going to be a "leader" at, selling drugs, breaking into cars, and robbing people, or could I shape my "destiny" in some positive way?

Well, the answer is yes but, to those of you who are reading this that think that it's "just a matter of choice" or that "anyone can do it…look at all the successful people that came from the ghetto," you are entirely wrong. Very wrong! Most people can't break the cycle they were thrown into; they can't overcome the environment, the abandonment, and the pressure to do like everyone else. It's not easy, and you shouldn't think it is. Suppose one's destiny is drugs, fighting, abusive relationships, and violence. In that case, it takes a lot to break that destiny, and most times, it takes a lot of help from others that have a genuine, selfless desire to see that one kid would grow up to be a remarkable person who is helping others in their lives.

I ask you to please lose the idea that most kids growing up as I did can overcome their destiny. It's just not true. I'm the

anomaly, the **exception** to the rule. I happened to have the right combination of genetic makeup, will, desire, and the right people at the right time to help me. If you genuinely want to see a change in a young man or woman, you first need to have the right desire. The intrinsic desire to see him or her become better, slowly, and surely. Secondly, you have to understand that everyone doesn't vibe with everyone. I had some incredible people who did care about me, but it may have been the wrong time or the wrong person at the wrong time. If you are working with youth, please recognize when YOU may not be the "right one" but, please don't just give up, and please stick with him or her until you help find the right person that can vibe on the same level as him or her.

The Cycle Is Broken

Overcoming this learned behavior was difficult, and the road wasn't just a straight one. It took time and effort, and I fell back, many times, into some of my old ways of thinking and being. But I kept growing. I kept trying to become a better person for myself and the two wonderful little kids I had now, oh yes, two kids now! My "Princess" daughter was born two years after my son. She was again planned, but boy was I young and inexperienced. I guess most new parents are inexperienced… hahaha. My ex and I tried and did our best in raising our children, and well, they turned out alright, so I guess we did well. Again, we went from Air Force Base to Air Force Base, experiencing some fantastic places.

I was "taken" away from my family like most military personnel for periods, but they had a wonderful mom that took great care of them. Even through the divorce, their mother kept them in mind, and I could never speak ill about her. Sometimes relationships don't work out, especially when you're seventeen and eighteen years old (I'm laughing on the inside… of course it wouldn't work out).

I continued to work on myself, travel, and absorb all the Air Force had to give to me. I was volunteering everywhere and teaching my love, martial arts. Things were amazing!

Another Stepping-Stone (A Huge Learning Opportunity)
After teaching martial arts in Hawaii for about three years, they moved us (stationed) to Cheyenne Mountain Air Force Base

(NORAD) in Colorado Springs, Colorado. Once I got settled into my new position, working for the base Commander, I decided to start teaching martial arts on Peterson Air Force Base. It didn't take long for me to gain students and to gain popularity around town. I wasn't just good as a martial artist, but I also had some business "knack." I think it was just my authentic personality that potential new students felt drawn to either that or my stunning good looks... hahaha.

So, it didn't take long; my school was thriving and safe. I was teaching on base, and it was going so well. I had zero risks because the Air Force Base and I would split the profit 80/20, and I had no rent or utility bills to pay. It seemed like a great idea and an excellent opportunity for me to do something I enjoy, teaching martial arts, and not having the risk of a full-time job or the hassle of renting a building. Until one day, I felt that I could do more, that I could make a more significant impact with martial arts. Martial arts were more than teaching someone how to defend themselves. It teaches people of all ages discipline, dedication, tenacity, drive, and creating an intrinsic desire to keep doing something until it's absolutely perfect, even if that means, hours on top of hours, doing the same thing again and again and again. That's what martial arts did for young Dave.

I had been toying with the idea of doing something bigger, affecting more people with what I had to offer. So, I moved my school off the Air Force base and into a community center in a low-income neighborhood. I thought I already had a big student base, and I thought I could make good money from that, so why not "give back" to the community. This turned out to be a colossal failure, I not only lost students from moving off base, but I quickly realized that poor people don't have a lot of drive or motive to get their kids into programs that could help them.

I know it sounds horrible, but it's an unfortunate truth in our inner cities. I paid for 2,000 flyers to pass out, walked from door to door, enlisted some of my teen students to do the same, discounted the monthly tuition for anyone in the neighborhood, and even had a scholarship program for three students a year. All they had to do was write a compelling essay as to how martial arts would help them.

Guess what, nothing at all, no new students, no scholarship submissions. It was utterly dead. Of course, this can create some self-doubt. Why? Am I not good enough? What did I do? Or what could I have done better? These were all questions I asked myself daily.

The only thing I could say to myself is that I tried, but trying wasn't paying the rent, and I was losing money every month, for months and months until fate kicked in.

One day after I taught the few students I had left, the director of the community center came up to me and said, "Hey Dave, there's a guy you have to meet. I think you and him have similar visions for at-risk youth. This guy, Jim, was renting space like I was at the community center. So, I found out what days he was there, and I popped in and introduced myself to him. Jim had a program for young men in foster homes, group homes, and juvenile detention centers. He was just starting up, and well, he was passionate about helping these young men. He and a couple of other mentors would gather the young men up from wherever they were "living" and bring them to the community center. They would have fellowship, talk about the Bible, about Jesus, and then play some physical games, like dodgeball, all together. I quickly said that I'd love to help and to see how we could collaborate.

Well, a year later, Brother Jim and I were thriving in our partnership and business. Jim's mentoring program had grown to the point where he worked programs and transitional apartments for the young men. He asked me to be the Vice President of his Board of Directors, and of course, I was thrilled to accept.

The impact I had with the young men in the program went from an individual impact to a significant impact on the entire program. Of course, I would never stop interacting and mentoring the young men in the program. The other side of the coin was that my martial arts program took off, I was gaining students, and I even developed a martial art mentoring program for the at-risk youth in our community. This was a dream come true for me - thriving Air Force career, thriving martial arts program for at-risk youth - and on top of all of this, my regular martial arts program took off, to where I moved from renting space at a community center to a store-front location on a major street, Garden of the Gods Road, in Colorado Springs. It was such an amazing time in my life.

I finally thought all my incredibly hard work and sacrifice had paid off. It was not just hard work on the business, but hard work on myself and who I really wanted to become. The martial arts school grew and grew and grew, and we had so many members that we went from a 1700 sq ft Dojo to a 10,000 sq ft school, and I was leasing part of it to a CrossFit instructor. Things were just amazing! I had plenty of students, I had instructors who taught me, and I lived my best life. Dreams do come true!

My Back, My Spine, My Spondylolisthesis!

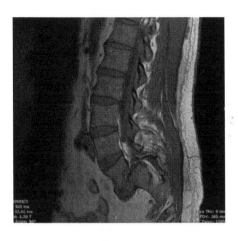

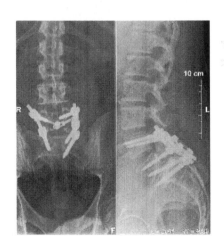

Just as my knee condition ended my career as a Security Forces Cop in the Air Force, before it even began, just so did my back end my dreams of being a superstar martial arts school owner and competitor. Spondylolisthesis, yeah, say that one ten times fast! Spondy, for short, is basically when your spine is broken. As you can see from the photos, something's not right... LOL. Well, my back had given me problems for years, but I thought it was just me being an "athlete." I worked out every day. I taught martial arts almost every day, plus football, rugby, and military stuff, so aches and pains were common all over. Until one day, I was lying on my couch, talking, and I was about to get up, and I couldn't. I couldn't walk! My legs just gave out on me. It was the strangest feeling I had ever felt. They didn't hurt. They just didn't work; my legs felt all tingly like they were asleep. I literally crawled upstairs to my bedroom, took some pills, and went to sleep. The next day I was able to walk, but my back did hurt.

I decided to make an appointment to see my doctor. He requested some X-rays of my back, and well, as I'm sitting at my desk at work, I get a phone call from my doctor. He said, "Can you come over to see me right now." NO ONE wants that call from their doctor! I immediately go over to the clinic to see him, and he shows me the X-ray of my spine. He had this baffled look on his face. He said, "Your spine is broken, and you need to see a specialist right away." I asked, "My spine is broken? WTF are you talking about?" Of course, this is my reaction. Well, since then, I've seen dozens of specialists, neurosurgeons, orthopedic doctors, psychical therapists, kinesthesiologists, and alternative medicine specialists, all over the world. Nothing seemed to help or work, and I was trying to avoid major spine surgery. But sometimes, "It is what it is." I had to give up on my dream of martial arts, and that probably has been the BIGGEST blow to me in my adult lifetime.

My "plan" was ruined! I retired from the Air Force, and for a couple of years, I was depressed. I was diagnosed with Major Depressive Disorder, and well, looking back, why wouldn't I be depressed. Not only am I not able to teach my passion, my love, I'm also retired from the Air Force, and that's new to me. So, after about two years of taking opioids and dealing with the pain and depression, I decided enough was enough and had a three-level spinal fusion. The surgery and recovery were rough, no joke, rough. And I wish I could say it was a success and that I'm all better. I'm not! Far from it but, I am a bit better than I was before surgery. I'm not popping pain pills all day, every day, so I'll take what I can get. I'm still hopeful that I'll continue to get better but, I'm 100% sure that I won't be teaching martial arts again. Of course, that makes me sad, but I've developed myself into the type of person who takes challenges head-on! So, now what's next.

What Happens After Your Dream (Comes Through)?

Again, as I sit writing this book, here in Greece, surrounded by, not just by a lovely house filled with nice things, an amazing and supportive wife but a heart filled with love for what I've been able to accomplish. I've been able to change my destiny, and I know it! I've been able to help so many people, and I'm grateful for it. I've become a life coach and a motivational speaker and directly see the change in the people I'm able to touch. For me, I feel complete. I know that I've not only tried, but I've also done, and so can you!

After I'm done with my book, I thought I would have accomplished all of my dreams. Overcoming destiny, getting over the baggage my life had left, joining the Air Force, and making it a twenty-four-year career, creating a mentoring program that has changed the lives of hundreds of young men, teaching martial arts to young and old, families and even other senior martial artists. But I keep finding ways to grow, challenge myself, and help humanity through my personal experiences.

A little over a year ago, one of my best friends, Ryan, and I created Unlimited Potential Network Academy (UPNA). It has taken shape and has been restructured over the last year. We went from wanting to mentor and coach young men on dating and self-confidence to what has morphed into a few areas that can help all sorts of people. I don't want to make my book a marketing tool so, if you're interested, go to www.upna.net or find me on social media, and we can talk. My point is, growth can and should be infinite; seeking knowledge, changing your opinion, or growing your point of view should be a constant in life. A person doesn't have to stay the same in any aspect of his or her life. We all can be better when we want to if we want to, but it is a lot of work, and often the most challenging work is against yourself. Some of us find ways to continue to challenge ourselves, to grow and develop. Complacency is not in our vocabulary, and nor do we want it to be.

Over the last year, I've gotten my degree in psychology, I've learned how to become a life coach, and I've refined my speaking style, and started a motivational YouTube channel, all the while enjoying the small steps I'm taking towards another and another and another life goal.

Becoming Better

No matter where you are in this big world, what "destiny" has thrown you into, you can become better. You can change your destiny. Many other motivational speakers and I are living proof of what one can do when you refuse. I mean, absolutely refuse to see anything else for your life. You don't know why you've been put on this earth yet, but I believe that so many people give up on themselves before they get to their "boiling point," that point in your life when you know you are changing your destiny to another more amazing one. There are so many excellent doctors, nurses, Presidents or Prime Ministers, Nobel Peace Prize winners or world shapers, like Dr. Martin Luther King, or Cristiano Ronaldo, out there, that never tap into their unlimited potential because it's hard; I mean fucking' hard to do it. But, you can, you can be the next Leonardo da Vinci, Mahatma Gandhi, Tony Stark (played by Robert Downey Jr.), or The Rock (Dwayne Johnson). Yes, all you have to do is believe you have something inside you that needs to come out. Know that it's hard work, not the hard work that most of us believe is "hard work" yes, you're going to put 15, 16, 17 hour days in, but that's not the type of hard work I mean. The hard work I'm talking about is overcoming yourself and your destiny, keeping that fire burning, no blazing, inside of you, no matter what. Don't let anyone or anything put that fire out. Every day, seek to be better, think, and feel better to believe better and pour the gas of desire onto that blazing fire within you. You can, and you will!

WHY ME?

From the Author

"I truly hope that this book finds its place in your heart and can help you in some way. I truly believe that I had to go through so much to help humanity better and bring people closer to true happiness within their lives." This is not a "feel-good book." It is a perspective book, it is a guidance book, and it is a real-life book. I will take you through a journey of my life and events within, but I also hope to give you the reader some enlightenment and tools to help you personally or help you better work with at-risk youth or adults.

What people have said...

"Sensei Dave saved my life. I was headed down a path that was going to lead me to be in prison, and now, I have the discipline and willpower to do well in my life."
(Young Mentee that is doing very well now)

"Mr. Armstrong, I would describe your speaking style as inspiring! The one-on-one attention you spend with the youth in our program was wonderful, and you were impactful. I would say you provide a casual and comfortable environment that promotes interactive communication. In addition, you have a professional yet down-to-earth approach that makes you a prime candidate for working with and influencing youth.
(Program Director, Big Brothers Big Sisters)

"Your speech at Lajes Air Base, Portugal, brought me to tears! I'm so glad to have been part of the audience you truly motivated me to start volunteering in our local community despite the language barrier." (U.S Air Force, General)

Testimonials

David Armstrong is a strong, compassionate, and charismatic person. He is the type of person to pick you up when you are feeling low and build you up to new heights. I do not mean this in terms of a close friend, on which we would all hope to have and rely. I mean this in terms of a stranger, an acquaintance, and a new person in your life. From the minute you meet Dave, you are drawn to his personality like a moth to a flame, but instead of burning up, you are then elevated to a new level of being. From his humility to his candor, from his genuine curiosity to his infectious positivity, David exudes not only what it means to be a good man, but a good human. Having known Dave for years and having seen, firsthand, the impact he has on people, it is truly inspiring to know him and to be a better person because of him. He selflessly shares his knowledge and experience with everyone. Willingly giving his trust to people who otherwise would not have any trust in anyone, and through doing this, mentors people of all ages and provides them a rock upon which to build themselves. While Dave may only count a handful of people as best friends, there are hundreds of people around the world who consider David theirs.

David was responsible for lifting me out of a depression after a failed marriage. Having only known me in passing and not being anywhere near to what I would consider close friends, it was he who sought me out and checked on me, and forced me to evaluate my mental wellbeing. Through his engagement, I was able to heal and grow and ultimately become a better

83

version of myself. Though we may not see eye to eye on all matters, I am eternally grateful to have his counsel and be at a position where I can voice my opinion openly and healthily. David Armstrong is a person of humble beginnings that hunted self-improvement as if his life depended on it. However, once he achieved it, he didn't stop there; he sought to help others like himself find or create their own opportunities to excel. If I only had one word to describe this man, it would be this - brother.

Colin J. Gerding (Warrant Officer, U.S. Army)

One quiet Sunday morning, someone was ringing the bell to our villa's gate. As I looked through the camera from the inside of our house, I noticed a man standing there. I asked him what he needed, and he asked for "Mr. Dave," I called Dave, and he opened the gate. As I noticed the man walking up our driving path toward the house, he was walking quite strangely. We didn't know who he was, and if he spoke English (we live in Greece), I asked him what he needed and translated from Greek to English his response. He said that he had heard of "Mr. Dave" and that he was a really nice guy in the area and that others told him to come and talk to Dave about something he needed. He needed surgery, urgently, but needed some more money to cover the surgery. He told Dave that some of the other neighbors and the Church helped him raise some of the money for the surgery but still needed some more. I remember I was very skeptical about whether this stranger was telling us the truth, because some of the pieces of the puzzle of his story were missing. I left Dave and the man to talk, but I heard as I walked

back inside the house that the man only wanted to borrow the money and that he would return it after the surgery. I still doubted what the guy was saying, but "Mr. Dave" had a different opinion. Dave gave him some money, and the man was super happy, looked thankful, and he promised to come back to return the money. I asked Dave if he believed him, and he said he wasn't sure also, but what if he was being honest?

A few months passed, and the man never came back. However, a couple of weeks ago, there he was again at the outside gate ringing the bell. This time, he was holding a small gas can, and as Dave came upstairs, I told him it was the stranger again and not even to bother to open the gate. Personally, I wouldn't have, but again, "Mr. Dave" had a different opinion. Not only did he open the gate, but he also let the guy in and talked with him for a while. This time the guy ran out of gas nearby and wanted some money to get some gas. What did "Mr. Dave" do? After he spoke with the man, for quite some time, he gave him some money and asked him if he wanted to come to do some yard work in our quite large yard. That was the agreement; the man got the money and promised Dave that he would come back on Sunday to do the yard. Three Sundays have passed now, and we haven't seen the man yet.

I asked Dave the other day if he wanted me to find someone else to do the yard, but I couldn't resist asking him how he felt that the stranger didn't come back to do the yard as he said. Dave answered, "I was almost sure he wouldn't come, but what if," another what if. That sums it up about Dave as he's writing this book; he only hopes one "What if" will help someone. Just one person would change their life because of him as he has changed mine completely for the last nine years. I will always admire the person he is, the heart he has, and the missions he sets out to accomplish. And what if all of his dreams come true?

Vasiliki Lappa-Armstrong (Amazing Wife)

The type of friend and person that will do anything for you without the expectation of anything in return. Big heart and truly cares!
Brock Schnute (U.S. Air Force)

Dave has spent a lot of his time doing outreach, and it was *through this generosity that I met him. A troubled teenager who was bitter at a broken system, I was at a crossroads. One way meant jail time, strife, and probably an early death, and the other way was the possibility of a fulfilling life. I was angry, undisciplined, and hurting. Constant let-downs by the people and the system that was supposed to protect me and help me be a better person left me with little hope of ever being "fixed." A long time interest of mine had been karate. Being a young kid and seeing Karate Kid, or The Three Ninjas, I had no idea what karate actually was, but I wanted to try. One of the outreach programs Dave did was teaching martial arts to troubled young men. Once a week at a community center, we would all meet, and for an hour before the meeting, we would have dojo time. It quickly became the highlight of the week, and I was always excited to go. But Dave didn't just teach martial arts; he taught life.*

For every instruction to have better form, there were wise words about applying lessons to real life (and no, it wasn't to beat up everyone else we didn't like). The importance of respect, discipline, tenacity, and sportsmanship was relayed with anecdotes and stories from his life. Even more than that, Dave understood us. He had been a young person in trouble and lost in the world. He didn't offer empty words and reassurances. Brutal honesty, when we messed up, was not always pleasant, but it was never condescending or mean spirited. That program transformed me. It gave me confidence in myself to be a better person. It gave me faith that if I worked hard, it would eventually pay off. It was literally this point in time I can say saved my life. I am honored, though, that a mentorship continued. I left the system to go home, and eventually, Dave moved away. However, he never stopped trying to help me be a better man. Whether it was grabbing me for lunch, or inviting me to help him move, or giving me free classes when I could make it to his dojo before he left. The encouragement never stopped. He is retired and living a life that he has earned. But I am proud to call him a friend and inspiration.

He changed my life with a totality that I struggle to find the words to convey. From a troubled teen destined for lock-up to a Paramedic that is heavily involved in helping my community and my profession. An angry, lost soul to a doting husband and incredibly proud father of two amazing boys. This is part of Dave's legacy. But you will never hear him say it, which is why I will. Dave is incredibly humble, but he has had impacts far greater than he will ever take credit for, and he has helped shape people who will further spread impacts. He is the ultimate success story, not because of how he lives, but because of how he has shaped the world around him.

Bryse Taylor (USA)

You don't have the power to make rainbows or waterfalls, sunsets, or roses, but you do have the power to bless people with your words and your smiles. Dave, you carry within you the power to make the world a little bit better. There is something utterly magnificent in you that I can't describe, but I truly love your uniqueness, my brother.
Vasilis Chronis (Greece)

I have more than a couple of amazing words!!!! I have watched you become one inspirational man. From the kid I hired who I knew had potential, to whom I see today shows what the human spirit can do when nourished...love you, Dave.
Barbara Lunnon Horzen (USA)

Inspiring... A lot of people had washed their hands of you, but my mom and I always believed in you. And look at you, so proud of you.
Keshia Johnson (Classmate, USA)

To the young and old Dave, my friend, I don't know if a couple of words will do. I'm familiar with the stomping grounds you and I have experienced, and I'm very proud and happy you have overcome this environment. Being comfortable and stagnant didn't hold you back. You chose to be a fighter, achiever, thinker, now motivator. Keep up the prosperous work. God bless you and all that your words touch.
Tosha Mayfield (Classmate, USA)

Frisbie Junior high... I just moved to Rialto. from Chicago- to live with my dad and stepmom. It was my 9th-grade year, and I knew that I was a misfit, and I embraced that. On my first day at FJH- I was sitting on the bench, alone. Up walks two guys, one was dressed like Randy "Macho Man" Savage, and the other one was dressed as a regular kid... In my mind, I was thinking, "who are these weirdos?" But the one that was dressed like Randy introduced himself as David, and the regular- dressed one was Charlie.

David's personality was so larger than life that everyone liked him, and those that didn't keep their mouths shut. Although David was the entertainer at school, his home life was quite different. Some mornings, we would all walk to school together, and all I knew was my best friend lived in a group home for boys. I didn't know why. I just thought that he was bad at one time, and now he wasn't. David made my time at Frisbie so much easier because he always had a smile and some crazy karate or wrestling moves, and regardless of what was going on in his life, he stayed positive. He always displayed courage under fire. I am forever grateful that God sent me such an awesome big brother. His story is an amazing story of strength, courage, and wisdom.

Kimberly Jones (Classmate, USA)

Despite all the obstacles life threw at Dave, he is a gentle, fun-loving, caring soul with a heart of gold. He possesses an ability to understand feelings better than most, therefore giving us simple spot-on solutions in how to deal with them in our everyday lives!

Tina DeLuca Tsourtsoulas (Greece)

Since the first time I met Dave, it was obvious how positive and fun to be around the guy he was. Everybody was gathering around him (especially the girls)! We started talking, and soon, after a while, we became friends and kept communication even though we were living in different countries. Until I heard of it, I hadn't realized while watching him enjoy his life full of experiences, friends, and luxury, how difficult his childhood had been. And how many shortcomings he overcame and what a Champion he was for having succeeded in taking control over

his circumstances and getting where he wanted to be! Cheers to the years and experiences to come, Brother. It's a great pleasure growing together!
Ryan Mitsogiannis (Athens, Greece)

If I had to use a word to describe Dave, I would pick resilient. We've known each other since grade school. His journey from a young man throughout adulthood has given him the ability to see the world for what it truly is or what it can be. Dave truly cares! His passion for helping teaches how to see things in a different way and enlightens one to be the best version of themselves!
Lori Smalls (Classmate, USA)

There are people who come into our lives to show us different perspectives. There are people who give us the strength to fight. There are people who believe more in us than we do in ourselves. Thank you, Dave! I will always remember when you told me - It will be painful, but you should become one with the pain and overcome it.
Tsvetana Cholakova (Sofia, Bulgaria)

Dave is an overcomer! He is a ball of energy and a positive life coach. He motivates and continues to inspire.
Virginia Hodges (USA)

We just need more Daves on our planet.
Vera Vang (USA)

Inspiration, teacher/mentor, compassionate, Great Friend.
Jacob Greenman (U.S. Air Force, USA)

Inspirational, motivational, and positive kind of guy!
Demitra Pappas (Greece)

I would say you are an inspiring, caring, loving person. You love to help people. You are a wonderful person who loves everyone.
Ginger Tucker (USA)

Motivated and straightforward with goals and inspiration.
Allan Abshire (Classmate, USA)

Funny, caring, full of life, and a positive energy guy with a lot of stories to tell.
Alexandra Arvaniti (Greece)

I honestly don't remember much from high school. Blocked a lot of that out, but one thing that always has stood out about you is your determination. You took your situation, and you overcame so much in life, and you are one of the most amazing inspirational, motivational, supportive people that I know. I do remember you and I walking together in our high school graduation, and I always remember you just being so positive and pushing me and always telling me to look for the good.
Stephanie McKinley (Classmate, USA)

Dave is a person whose life is truly a testimony of real experiences that conformed him into a teacher of

determination, edification, and inspiration to everyone with whom he comes in contact! Dave's life story motivates and pushes others to be the best; they can be, no matter how hard it gets sometimes. He has been just that for me, both inside the dojo and out in the real world! A man truly sensitive to the spirit and filled with a real love for life!
Scott Daily (USA)

It's been a whirlwind. I just want to say thank you for the video. You've no idea how much your words resonate with me. When I listen to you, talk it's not just like scrolling on any video, I am captivated by your energy and feel this overwhelming sense of relief each time I hit a video that hits home with the current circumstance.
Kelly (UK)

Dave is a class act! From day one, he was an inspiration and took the time to know me!
Ninfa (U.S. Air Force)

Dave Armstrong is a man that desires to have a positive influence on anyone with whom he comes into contact. He takes the time to keep those who are struggling or going through hard times in good spirits. It is always a joy to be around such a great individual, not because of his accomplishments but because of his character.

Khadir Truth (U.S. Air Force)

ABOUT THE AUTHOR
ABOUT THE AUTHOR

Sensei Dave Armstrong
Motivational Speaker
Life Coach
Mentor
Unlimited Potential Network Academy

Sensei Dave Armstrong was a product of a broken family, foster care, youth correction facilities, and a deceased, only parent at the age of thirteen. As an "at-risk" youth and a "product" of the inner-city educational system, young Sensei Dave was predestined to run with gangs, not graduate high school and be dead or in jail by the age of eighteen. After his mother passed away, Sensei Dave lost all contact with his family and was in and out of boys homes, juvenile detention, and foster homes in California until he turned eighteen and "transitioned" out of state custody. But along the way, he was influenced by many amazing people, two of which were: his CASA, Ron Barnick, an Air Force pilot, and Sensei Otto Johnson, his first martial arts instructor. Without their mentoring, Sensei Dave Armstrong would not have been able to mentor, guide, help, and motivate the thousands of youth, mentors, foster parents, and humanity as he has done for years now.

Sensei Dave is now retired after twenty-four years of service to our country in the U.S. Air Force. He has also sat on the Board of Directors as Vice President for non-profit organizations, created his own Martial Arts Mentoring program, and owned three martial arts schools in the United States. As a U.S. Air Force Veteran, Sensei Dave has been able to travel and see the world, spreading his positive and motivational personality from country to country. Currently, Sensei Dave is a Professional Life Coach and Motivational Speaker and tours around the United States and Europe, helping individuals and companies achieve their personal and professional goals.

Travel the W🌐rld with Friends!